World *of* Reptiles

World *of*

Reptiles

Introducing the World of Reptiles

Venomous snakes and deadly crocodiles tend to be the reptiles which capture the imagination of most people, but the diversity of the planet's reptiles is so much greater than this, with many of the smaller and less well-known species being of equal or greater interest than their famous relatives.

World of Reptiles is a visual celebration of the planet's varied and amazing reptilian life. At present there are estimated to be around 10,800 reptile species from 86 families – from oceanic Leatherback Turtles to subterranean Blind Snakes – utilising almost every habitat available.

The book contains 240 images covering more than 220 species from 68 of these families, in order to depict as wide a diversity as possible of reptiles worldwide. The pictures have been selected in order to show the varied nature of reptile forms, encompassing Turtles, Tuataras, Lizards, Snakes, Amphisbaenians and Crocodiles, and the range of interesting things they do, such as hunting, hiding, feeding, displaying, hatching and much more. In some cases they show the reptiles in the context of the landscape of their natural habitat, while in others they depict a very rare species or family that may rarely, if ever, have been included in a book before.

Estimates of the exact number of reptile species vary according to the latest studies, and are changing all the time as we learn more, but for the sake of giving some order to the images *World of Reptiles* has adopted taxonomy and nomenclature recommended by The Reptile Database (www.reptile-database.org) as the basis for the listing.

Above all, we hope that you enjoy this book and its amazing images, and that it contributes towards inspiring further interest in reptiles and their conservation worldwide.

TURTLES

Alligator Snapping Turtle *Macrochelys temminckii*
USA

Common Snapping Turtle *Chelydra serpentina*
NORTH AMERICA

European Pond Turtle *Emys orbicularis*
EURASIA

Galápagos Tortoise *Chelonoidis nigra*
GALÁPAGOS ISLANDS

Galápagos Tortoise *Chelonoidis nigra*
GALÁPAGOS ISLANDS

Aldabra Giant Tortoise *Aldabrachelys gigantean*

SEYCHELLES

Leopard Tortoise *Stigmochelys pardalis*
AFRICA

African Spurred Tortoise *Geochelone sulcata*
AFRICA

Reeves' Turtle *Mauremys reevesii*

Pig-nosed Turtle *Carettochelys insculpta*

AUSTRALIA AND NEW GUINEA

Texas Spiny Softshell Turtle *Apalone spinifera emoryi*

USA

White-lipped Mud Turtle *Kinosternon leucostomum*

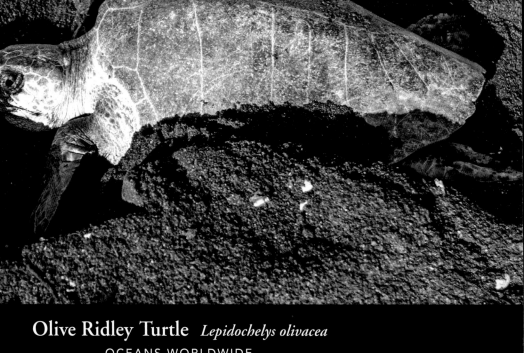

Olive Ridley Turtle *Lepidochelys olivacea*

OCEANS WORLDWIDE

Green Turtle *Chelonia mydas*
OCEANS WORLDWIDE

Hawksbill Turtle *Eretmochelys imbricata*

Leatherback Turtle *Dermochelys coriacea*

OCEANS WORLDWIDE

Northern Snake-necked Turtle *Chelodina oblonga*
AUSTRALIA

Mata Mata *Chelus fimbriatus*
SOUTH AMERICA

African Helmeted Turtle *Pelomedusa subrufa*

Big-headed Amazon River Turtle *Peltocephalus dumerilianus*
SOUTH AMERICA

Yellow-spotted River Turtle *Podocnemis unifilis*
SOUTH AMERICA

Arrau Turtle *Podocnemis expansa*
SOUTH AMERICA

TUATARAS

Northern Tuatara *Sphenodon punctatus punctatus*
NEW ZEALAND

Brothers Island Tuatara *Sphenodon punctatus guntheri*
NEW ZEALAND

Common Agama or **Rainbow Agama** *Agama agama*
AFRICA

Black-necked Agama or **Blue-headed Tree Agama** *Acanthocercus atricollis*
AFRICA

Starred Agama *Stellagama stellio*
SOUTH-EAST EUROPE AND SOUTH-WEST ASIA

Caucasian Agama *Paralaudakia caucasia*
SOUTH-WEST ASIA

Frill-necked Lizard *Chlamydosaurus kingii*
AUSTRALIA

Central Bearded Dragon *Pogona vitticeps*
AUSTRALIA

Boyd's Forest Dragon *Lophosaurus boydii*
AUSTRALIA

Thorny Devil *Moloch horridus*
AUSTRALIA

Sulawesi Lined Flying Lizard *Draco spilonotus*
INDONESIA

Fan-throated Lizard *Sitana ponticeriana*
SOUTH ASIA

Panther Chameleon *Furcifer pardalis*
MADAGASCAR

Namaqua Dwarf Chameleon *Bradypodion occidentale*

Veiled Chameleon · *Chamaeleo calyptratus*

ARABIA

Veiled Chameleon *Chamaeleo calyptratus*
ARABIA

Namaqua Chameleon *Chamaeleo namaquensis*
SOUTHERN AFRICA

Fischer's Chameleon *Kinyongia fischeri*
TANZANIA

Kenya Pygmy Chameleon *Rieppeleon kerstenii*
EAST AFRICA

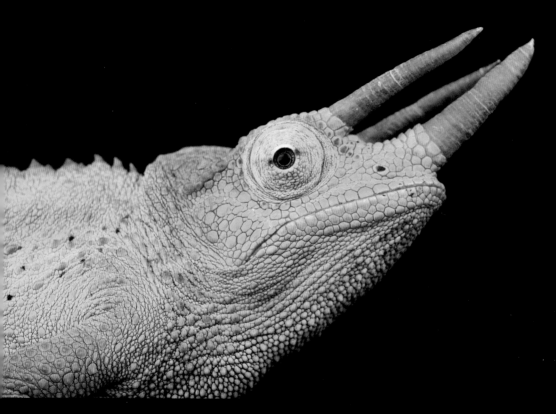

Jackson's Chameleon *Trioceros jacksonii*
EAST AFRICA

Brown Leaf Chameleon *Brookesia superciliaris*
MADAGASCAR

Minute Leaf Chameleon *Brookesia minima*
MADAGASCAR

Plumed Basilisk *Basiliscus plumifrons*

CENTRAL AMERICA

Hernandez's Helmeted Basilisk *Corytophanes hernandesii*
MEXICO

Marine Iguana *Amblyrhynchus cristatus*

GALÁPAGOS ISLANDS

Marine Iguana *Amblyrhynchus cristatus*
GALÁPAGOS ISLANDS

Galápagos Land Iguana *Conolophus subcristatus*
GALÁPAGOS ISLANDS

Fiji Crested Iguana *Brachylophus vitiensis*
FIJI

Black Spiny-tailed Iguana *Ctenosaura similis*

Cuban Rock Iguana *Cyclura nubila*
CUBA

Desert Iguana *Dipsosaurus dorsalis*
NORTH AMERICA

Green Iguana *Iguana iguana*

SOUTH AMERICA, CENTRAL AMERICA AND THE CARIBBEAN

Chuckwalla *Sauromalus ater*

NORTH AMERICA

Green Tree Lizard *Enyalius iheringi*

Madagascan Collared Iguana *Oplurus cuvieri*

Common Collared Lizard *Crotaphytus collaris*

NORTH AMERICA

Texas Horned Lizard *Phrynosoma cornutum*
NORTH AMERICA

Knight Anole *Anolis equestris*
CUBA

Green Anole *Anolis carolinensis*
NORTH AMERICA

Red-eyed Wood Lizard *Enylioides oshaughnessyi*
SOUTH AMERICA

Western Leaf Lizard *Stenocercus fimbriatus*
SOUTH AMERICA

Cuban Curlytail Lizard *Leiocephalus cubensis*

CUBA

Fabian's Lizard *Liolaemus fabiani*

Satanic Leaf-tailed Gecko *Uroplatus phantasticus*
MADAGASCAR

Tokay Gecko *Gekko gekko*

Mediterranean House Gecko *Hemidactylus turcicus*

MEDITERRANEAN

Cat Gecko *Aeluroscalabotes felinus*
SOUTH-EAST ASIA

Leopard Gecko *Eublepharis macularius*
SOUTH ASIA

Northern Spiny-tailed Gecko *Strophurus ciliaris*
AUSTRALIA

Main's Ground Gecko *Lucasium mainii*
AUSTRALIA

Ragazzi's Fan-footed Gecko *Ptyodactylus ragazzi*
AFRICA

Wonder Gecko *Teratoscincus scincus*
ASIA

Thick-tailed Gecko *Underwoodisaurus milii*

Burton's Legless Lizard *Lialis burtonis*
AUSTRALIA

Papua Legless Lizard *Lialis jicari*
NEW GUINEA

Sungazer or **Giant Girdled Lizard** *Smaug giganteus*
SOUTH AFRICA

Common Flat Lizard *Platysaurus intermedius*

Giant Plated Lizard *Gerrhosaurus validus*
AFRICA

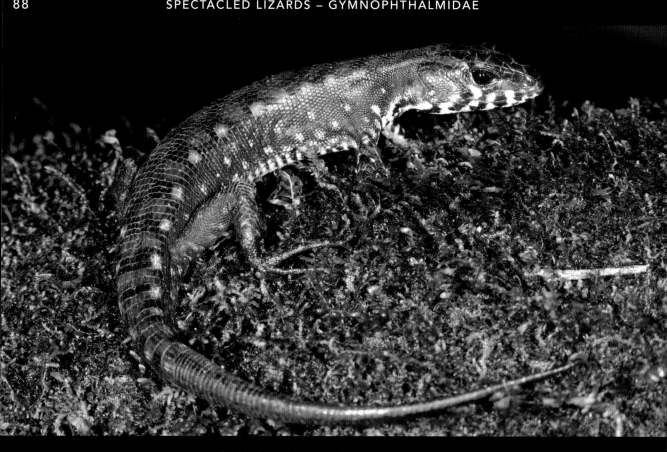

Gymnophthalmid lizard species *Potamites* sp.

SOUTH AMERICA

Western Whiptail *Aspidoscelis tigris*
SOUTH AMERICA

Crocodile Tegu *Crocodilurus amazonicus*
SOUTH AMERICA

Northern Caiman Lizard *Dracaena guianensis*

SOUTH AMERICA

Black-and-white Tegu *Tupinambis merianae*
SOUTH AMERICA

Tenerife Lizard *Gallotia galloti*

CANARY ISLANDS

Blue-tailed Sandveld Lizard *Nucras caesicaudata*
AFRICA

Sand Lizard *Lacerta agilis*

EURASIA

Milos Wall Lizard *Podarcis milensis*
GREECE

Common Lizard *Zootoca vivipara*

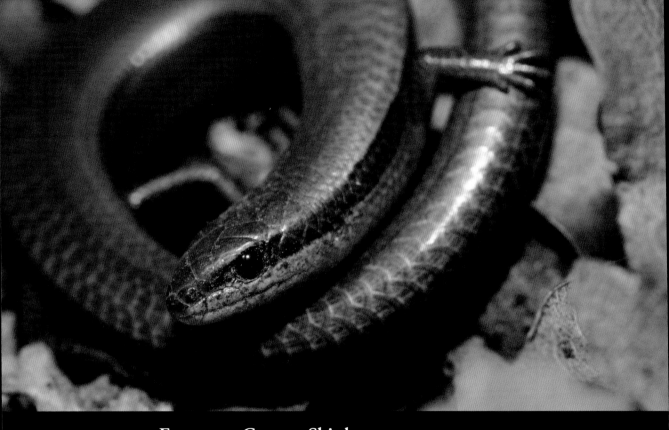

European Copper Skink *Ablepharus kitaibelii*
EURASIA

Red-eyed Crocodile Skink *Tribolonotus gracilis*

Shingleback *Tiliqua rugosa*
AUSTRALIA

Common Sun Skink *Eutropis multifasciata*
SOUTH ASIA

Pygmy Spiny-tailed Skink *Egernia depressa*
AUSTRALIA

Desert Lidless Skink *Ablepharus deserti*

Yellow-spotted Night Lizard *Lepidophyma flavimaculatum*
CENTRAL AMERICA

Slow-worm *Anguis fragilis*
EURASIA

Hispaniolan Giant Galliwasp *Celestus warreni*
HISPANIOLA

Texas Alligator Lizard *Gerrhonotus infernalis*
NORTH AMERICA

California Legless Lizard *Anniella pulchra*
NORTH AMERICA

Newman's Knob-scaled Lizard *Xenosaurus newmanorum*
MEXICO

Gila Monster *Heloderma suspectum*

MEXICO AND USA

Earless Monitor Lizard *Lanthanotus borneensis*
BORNEO

Komodo Dragon *Varanus komodoensis*

Komodo Dragon *Varanus komodoensis*
INDONESIA

Lace Monitor or **Lace Goanna** *Varanus varius*
AUSTRALIA

Bengal Monitor *Varanus bengalensis*
SOUTH ASIA

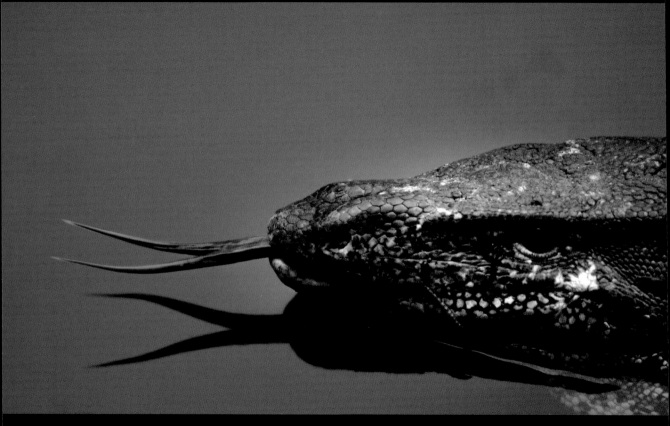

Asian Water Monitor *Varanus salvator*
SOUTH ASIA

Nile Monitor *Varanus niloticus*
AFRICA

AMPHISBAENIANS

Wedge-snouted Worm Lizard *Monopeltis decosteri*
AFRICA

Zarudny's Worm Lizard *Diplometopon zarudnyi*
SOUTH-WEST ASIA

SNAKES

Javan File Snake or **Elephant Trunk Snake** *Acrochordus javanicus*
SOUTH ASIA

Little File Snake *Acrochordus granulatus*

SOUTH ASIA AND NORTH AUSTRALIA

American Pipe Snake or **False Coral Snake** *Anilius scytale*

Southern Stiletto Snake *Atractaspis bibronii*
AFRICA

Variable Burrowing Asp *Atractaspis irregularis*
AFRICA

Striped Quill-snouted Snake *Xenocalamus bicolor lineatus*

AFRICA

Northern Boa *Boa imperator*

MEXICO, CENTRAL AMERICA AND SOUTH AMERICA

Boa Constrictor *Boa constrictor*
SOUTH AMERICA

Pacific Tree Boa *Candoia bibroni*
MELANESIA AND POLYNESIA

Emerald Tree Boa *Corallus caninus*

Rainbow Boa *Epicrates cenchria*
CENTRAL AMERICA AND SOUTH AMERICA

Yellow Anaconda *Eunectes notaeus*
SOUTH AMERICA

Rubber Boa *Charina bottae*

NORTH AMERICA

Rosy Boa *Lichanura trivirgata*
NORTH AMERICA

Javelin Sand Boa *Eryx jaculus*
EURASIA AND NORTH AFRICA

Rainbow Water Snake *Enhydris enhydris*
SOUTH ASIA

White-bellied Mangrove Snake *Fordonia leucobalia*
SOUTH ASIA AND NORTH AUSTRALIA

Puff-faced Water Snake *Homalopsis buccata*
SOUTH ASIA

Dragon Snake *Xenodermus javanicus*
SOUTH ASIA

Perrotet's Mountain Snake *Xylophis perroteti*
INDIA

Blunt-headed Slug Snake *Aplopeltura boa*
SOUTH ASIA

Aurora House Snake *Lamprophis aurora*

AFRICA

Brown House Snake *Lamprophis fuliginosus*
AFRICA

Common Brown Water Snake *Lycodonomorphus rufulus*

Mole Snake *Pseudaspis cana*

AFRICA

Variegated Slug-eater *Duberria variegata*
SOUTHERN AFRICA

Cinnabar Malagasy Vinesnake *Ithycyphus miniatus*

Malagasy Leaf-nosed Snake *Langaha madagascariensis*
MADAGASCAR

Malagasy Hog-nosed Snake *Leioheterodon madagascariensis*

Malagasy Cat-eyed Snake *Madagascarophis meridionalis*

Water Rhabdops *Rhabdops aquaticus*
INDIA

False Smooth Snake *Macroprotodon cucullatus*
MEDITERRANEAN

Oriental Whipsnake *Ahaetulla prasina*
SOUTH ASIA

Banded Racer *Argyrogena fasciolata*

INDIAN SUBCONTINENT

Glossy Snake *Arizona elegans*
NORTH AMERICA

Trans-Pecos Rat Snake *Bogertophis subocularis*
NORTH AMERICA

Black-headed Cat Snake *Boiga nigriceps*
SOUTH ASIA

Scarlet Snake *Cemophora coccinea*
NORTH AMERICA

Mojave Shovel-nosed Snake *Chionactis occipitalis occipitalis*
NORTH AMERICA

Wagler's Sipo *Chironius scurrulus*
SOUTH AMERICA

Golden Tree Snake *Chrysopelea ornata*
SOUTH ASIA

Western Whipsnake *Hierophis viridiflavus*
SOUTHERN EUROPE

Southern Black Racer *Coluber constrictor priapus*
NORTH AMERICA

Smooth Snake *Coronella austriaca*

EURASIA

Red-lipped Snake *Crotaphopeltis hotamboeia*
AFRICA

Rhombic Egg-eater *Dasypeltis scabra*

AFRICA AND ARABIA

Nganson Bronzeback *Dendrelaphis ngansonensis*
SOUTH ASIA

South American Forest Racer *Dendrophidion percarinatum*

CENTRAL AMERICA AND SOUTH AMERICA

Red-banded Snake or **Sakishima Odd-tooth Snake** *Dinodon rufozomatus walli*
JAPAN

Boomslang *Dispholidus typus*
AFRICA

Eastern Indigo Snake *Drymarchon couperi*
NORTH AMERICA

Speckled Racer *Drymobius margaritiferus*
NORTH AMERICA AND CENTRAL AMERICA

Aesculapian Snake *Zamenis longissimus*

Eastern Milksnake *Lampropeltis triangulum*
NORTH AMERICA

Parrot Snake *Leptophis ahaetulla*

CENTRAL AMERICA AND SOUTH AMERICA

Striped Racer *Masticophis lateralis*
NORTH AMERICA

Rough Green Snake *Opheodrys aestivus*

Brown Vinesnake *Oxybelis aeneus*

AMERICAS

Saddled Leafnose Snake *Phyllorhynchus browni*
NORTH AMERICA

Pacific Gopher Snake *Pituophis catenifer*
NORTH AMERICA

Longnose Snake　*Rhinocheilus lecontei*

NORTH AMERICA

Peninsular (Green) Rat Snake *Senticolis triaspis*
NORTH AMERICA AND CENTRAL AMERICA

Twig Snake *Thelotornis capensis*
AFRICA

California Lyre Snake *Trimorphodon lyrophanes*

European Grass Snake *Natrix natrix*

Red-sided Garter Snake *Thamnophis sirtalis parietalis*
NORTH AMERICA

Smooth Earth Snake *Virginia valeriae*
NORTH AMERICA

Cope's Black-striped Snake *Coniophanes piceivittis*

Night Snake *Hypsiglena torquata*
MEXICO

Northern Cat-eyed Snake *Leptodeira septentrionalis*
CENTRAL AMERICA AND SOUTH AMERICA

Cloudy Snail-eating Snake *Sibon nebulatus*
SOUTH AMERICA

Eastern Wormsnake *Carphophis amoenus*
NORTH AMERICA

Pacific Ringneck Snake *Diadophis punctatus amabilis*
NORTH AMERICA

Military Ground Snake *Erythrolamprus miliaris*
SOUTH AMERICA

Western Hognose Snake *Heterodon nasicus*
NORTH AMERICA

Red-tailed Pipe Snake *Cylindrophis ruffus*
SOUTH ASIA

Desert Death Adder *Acanthophis pyrrhus*
AUSTRALIA

Red-headed Krait *Bungarus flaviceps*
SOUTH ASIA

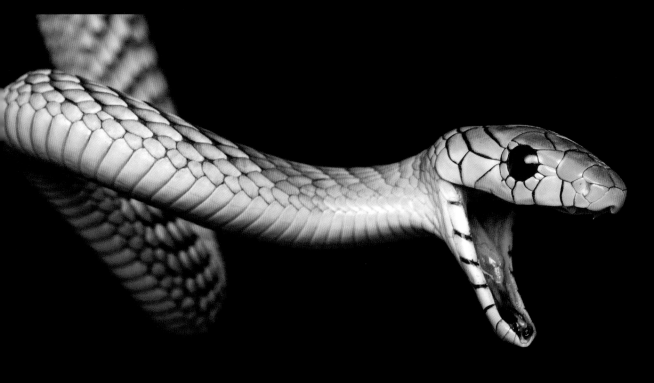

Western Green Mamba *Dendroaspis viridis*
WEST AFRICA

Black Mamba *Dendroaspis polylepis*

AFRICA

Rinkhals *Hemachatus haemachatus*

SOUTHERN AFRICA

Sonoran Coral Snake *Micruroides euryxanthus*
NORTH AMERICA

Eastern Coral Snake *Micrurus fulvius*
NORTH AMERICA

Cape Cobra *Naja nivea*
AFRICA

Indian Cobra *Naja naja*
INDIAN SUBCONTINENT

Tiger Snake *Notechis scutatus*

AUSTRALIA

King Cobra *Ophiophagus hannah*

Inland Taipan *Oxyuranus microlepidotus*
AUSTRALIA

Red-bellied Black Snake *Pseudechis porphyriacus*
AUSTRALIA

Eastern Brown Snake *Pseudonaja textilis*
AUSTRALIA

Hook-nosed Sea Snake *Hydrophis schistosus*

SEAS OFF SOUTH ASIA AND AUSTRALIA

Yellow-lipped Sea Krait *Laticauda colubrina*
INDIAN OCEAN AND PACIFIC OCEAN

Black-headed Python *Aspidites melanocephalus*

Jungle Carpet Python *Morelia spilota cheynei*
AUSTRALIA

Green Tree Python *Morelia viridis*

INDONESIA, NEW GUINEA AND AUSTRALIA

Reticulated Python *Malayopython reticulatus*

SOUTH-EAST ASIA

Burmese Python *Python bivittatus*
SOUTH ASIA

Royal Python or **Ball Python** *Python regius*
AFRICA

Dusky Dwarf Boa *Tropidophis melanurus*
CUBA

Elliot's Shieldtail *Uropeltis ellioti*
INDIA

Common Night Adder *Causus rhombeatus*
AFRICA

Eyelash Viper *Bothriechis schlegelii*
CENTRAL AMERICA AND SOUTH AMERICA

Jararaca *Bothrops jararaca*
SOUTH AMERICA

Malayan Pit Viper *Calloselasma rhodostoma*
SOUTH-EAST ASIA

Black-tailed Rattlesnake *Crotalus molossus*
NORTH AMERICA

Bushmaster *Lachesis muta*
SOUTH AMERICA

Hognosed Pitviper *Porthidium nasutum*
CENTRAL AMERICA AND SOUTH AMERICA

Sabah Bamboo Pitviper *Trimeresurus sabahi*
SOUTH-EAST ASIA

Bush Viper *Atheris squamigera*

Great Lakes Bush Viper *Atheris nitschei*
AFRICA

Gaboon Viper *Bitis rhinoceros*
AFRICA

Puff Adder *Bitis arietans*
AFRICA

Desert Horned Viper *Cerastes cerastes*

AFRICA AND ARABIA

Russell's Viper *Daboia russelii*
INDIAN SUBCONTINENT

Saw-scaled Viper *Echis carinatus*

SOUTH ASIA

Eurasian Adder *Vipera berus*
EURASIA

Nose-horned Viper *Vipera ammodytes*
EUROPE

Sunbeam Snake *Xenopeltis unicolor*

SOUTH-EAST ASIA

Eurasian Blind Snake *Typhlops vermicularis*
EURASIA

Brahminy Blind Snake *Ramphotyphlops braminus*
AFRICA AND ASIA

Blotched Blind Snake *Afrotyphlops congestus*
AFRICA

CROCODILES

Spectacled Caiman *Caiman crocodilus*
CENTRAL AMERICA AND SOUTH AMERICA

American Alligator *Alligator mississippiensis*

Black Caiman *Caiman niger*

SOUTH AMERICA

Cuvier's Dwarf Caiman *Paleosuchus palpebrosus*
SOUTH AMERICA

Nile Crocodile *Crocodylus niloticus*

AFRICA

Nile Crocodile *Crocodylus niloticus*
AFRICA

American Crocodile *Crocodylus acutus*

AMERICAS

Slender-snouted Crocodile *Mecistops cataphractus*
AFRICA

Gharial *Gavialis gangeticus*

A Complete Guide to Reptiles of Australia
Fifth Edition
Steve Wilson and Gerry Swan
ISBN 978 1 92554 602 6

A Field Guide to Reptiles of New South Wales
Third Edition
Gerry Swan, Ross Sadlier and Glenn Shea
ISBN 978 1 92554 608 8

A Field Guide to Reptiles of Queensland
Second Edition
Steve Wilson
ISBN 978 1 92151 748 8

A Year in British Wildlife
Mark Ward
ISBN 978 1 92554 611 8

Australian Wildlife On Your Doorstep
Stephanie Jackson
ISBN 978 1 92554 630 9

Crocodiles of the World
Colin Stevenson
ISBN 978 1 92554 628 6

Extreme Animals
Dominic Couzens
ISBN 978 1 92554 649 1

Reed Concise Guide: Snakes of Australia
Gerry Swan
ISBN 978 1 92151 789 1

Reed Mini Guide to Animals [of Britain]
Reptiles • Amphibians • Mammals
Marianne Taylor
ISBN 978 1 92554 624 8

World's Most Endangered
Sophie McCallum
ISBN 978 1 92554 627 9

In the same series as this title:
World of Birds
ISBN 978 1 92554 652 1

For details of these books and hundreds of other
Natural History titles see
www.newhollandpublishers.com
and follow ReedNewHolland
on Facebook and Instagram

First published in 2019 by Reed New Holland Publishers
London • Sydney • Auckland

Bentinck House, 3–8 Bolsover Street, London W1W 6AB, UK
1/66 Gibbes Street, Chatswood, NSW 2067, Australia
5/39 Woodside Avenue, Northcote, Auckland 0627, New Zealand

www.newhollandpublishers.com

A record of this book is held at the British Library and the National Library of Australia.

ISBN 978 1 92554 653 8

Group Managing Director: Fiona Schultz
Publisher and Project Editor: Simon Papps
Designer: Andrew Davies
Production Director: Arlene Gippert
Printer: Toppan Leefung Printing Limited

10 9 8 7 6 5 4 3 2 1

Keep up with Reed New Holland
and New Holland Publishers on Facebook
www.facebook.com/ReedNewHolland
www.facebook.com/NewHollandPublishers

Front cover: European Green Lizard *Lacerta viridis* (Lacertidae).
Back cover: Hawksbill Turtle *Eretmochelys imbricata* (Cheloniidae).
Page 1: Crocodilian eye (Alligatoridae or Crocodylidae).
Pages 2–3: Panther Chameleon *Furcifer pardalis* (Chamaeleonidae).
Page 8: Marine Iguana *Amblyrhynchus cristatus* (Iguanidae).